On the Other Side of This Reality

Gregory Edward Douglas

PEGASUS BOOKS

Pegasus Books
8165 Valley Green Drive
Sacramento, CA 95823
www.pegasusbooks.net

First Edition: July 2020

Published in North America by Pegasus Books. For information, please contact Pegasus Books c/o Marcus McGee, 8165 Valley Green Drive, Sacramento, CA 95823.

Library of Congress Cataloguing-In-Publication Data
Gregory Edward Douglas
On the Other Side of This Reality/ Gregory Edward Douglas – 1st ed.
p. cm.
Library of Congress Control Number: 2010943597
ISBN – 978-1-941859-81-0
1. POLITICAL SCIENCE / Civil Rights. 2. POLITICAL SCIENCE / Political Ideologies. 3. SOCIAL SCIENCE / African American Studies.4. SOCIAL SCIENCE / Discrimination. 5. POLITICAL SCIENCE / Public Policy / Social Policy.

10 9 8 7 6 5 4 3 2 1

Comments about *On the Other Side of This Reality* and requests for additional copies, book club rates and author speaking appearances may be addressed to Pegasus Books c/o Gregory Edward Douglas, or you can send your comments and requests via e-mail to gregdouglas767@icloud.com.

Also available as an eBook from Internet retailers and from Pegasus Books

Printed in the United States of America

This book is dedicated to the us

of the here and now

In the hope that we may

regain our full faces

discover our smiles again

speak with unfiltered voices

approach even closer

than at arms length

be able to touch again

and hug one another

Or

has the evolution of this world

taken us

from flat

to round to

trap-&-void...

gregoryedouglas
seven/three/cleareyesight

On the Other Side of This Reality

I wrote *On the Other Side of This Reality* to illustrate that you and I have continued to develop a tolerance for the intolerable injustice meted out over a period that seems like almost forever. This is too eerie. In avoiding controversy and confrontations regarding segregation and racism, we have allowed ourselves to be cornered and suffocated. We have reserved that air for others to garner the energy and forge agendas, which are not only foreign to our beliefs, but they are alien to our livelihoods. We pause and guess when innately we should speak out and act.

The allegiance of our cops and courts are unnerving and have stonewalled our efforts by controlling the narrative, principally because this juggernaut is only concerned with the concept of self-preservation, where the definition of justice is about winning and not about right or wrong. And so we find ourselves continually trudging through the same old ruts in the road, over and over and over again.

We speak out only when the impact of our indignation, that pebble in our shoe, becomes far too painful to take another step. Disastrously, our reactions are postscripts for the deaths of Black Brothers and Black Sisters, and our tears and gut-wrenching screams serve neither as deterrents, comforts nor as solutions. The transparency of this "system," through iPhones and body cams have brought into full view the defenselessness of its black victims and the vicious unabated disregard for life in those sworn to uphold the law.

The Covid-19 coronavirus presents us with another formidable opponent and with even more questions than answers. The rigid protocols that were put into place, when not heeded, have yielded a mortality rate to equal that of a major war. How could something so invisible impact the world, its economies, and more importantly, its people—as devastatingly as it has?

Factor in Covid's higher mortality rate and its prevalence for Black People, along with the police and judicial inequities, and the temperature of the Black communities have come to a boiling point. This tests the veracity of a constitution that, in regard to its attention and care for Blacks in areas of equality, protection and health issues have been found lacking. If in truth, the tenets of the constitution and its elected officials cannot rectify these problems for all of its peoples, then it is obliged, by its own ideals, to have us, We The People, seek other solutions.

Gregory Edward Douglas

Title List

When Wars Go Viral

Old timers can tell you
That they could hear this resounding
Volley of Thunder
First creeping then bounding over the horizon
With its ear-splitting earth trembling approach
Balls of fire smoke and dust
Choked out the sky
Whistling projectiles
Drew blood amputations and worse
That war gasped for reason and pled for relief
As the days struggled to meet midnights
Even atheists bowed their heads
Afraid to ask but begging to know
If they would see tomorrow...
Today
The neophytes and young recruits can tell you
Of the fifth columns' masterful insurgents
Hushed in tracheal trenches and
Concealed in bronchial bunkers
Raising temperatures
And then with a heralding cough
As its battle cry
Launching salvos of nano projectiles

Until spasmodic constrictions choke out the lungs

This war for our air gasps for relief

For vents to vent – to ease whiteouts' shrill cry

As the day struggles to meet midnight

Even atheists bow their heads

Afraid to ask but begging to know

If we will see tomorrow...

gregorye.douglas
three/thirty/2020

A Covid Day in Tiferet's Coffee House

I passed by
your window today
just like yesterday
and the day before
viewing sophisticated ghosts
burying their heads
in newspapers and novels
lifting cups
with perfectly
weightless pinkies
pointlessly pointed
towards the ceiling
perhaps reflecting
an attitude of
post coffee, expresso
or post mocha
contentment

The counter offers
your ever-pleasant smile
Its intractable beam
induces them to buy more
and tarry even longer
to sip not chug
with napkin in lap
to capture
muffin crumbs
that escape
loose lips
which efficiently
serve for sips
then sends
them on their way
through closed doors
yes, until tomorrow

gregorye.douglas
four/twenty-three/2020

Grans of the Covid Born

Photographed
We held our breath
As you exhaled
With this long loud lusty cry
Creating the vacuum
That made room for your soul
As you took your
First swim in air
To mark your arrival
Initially – We were afraid to hold you
Hand crafting hearts & ghost hugs
Synthetic love behind plexiglass
As the masks held us & Covid-19 at bay

Maiden Flights normally elate us
How heart-rendering
The threat of Covid illness
In births deflate us
This Covid-19 separates us

Lowering the spectrum of our expectations

Drawing anxious cloud cover

Hindering hopes & our aspirations

& behind this plexiglass

Along with the kisses & fingerprints

Are prayers in fervent search for solutions

That will gift us with the resolutions

So I may hold you, my precious loved one

Unhindered & without hesitation

Yes – even before your first words embrace me...

gregorye.douglas
four/Thirty/cleareyesight

The March

Although we may empathize
And sympathize
Over 100,000 foreigners,
Friends and families' fatalities
We also need to lift up your heads
Pray and give God the Glory
For keeping us safe
Out of harm's way
In this sad heart-breaking story
And for giving us the power
To be able to fight on
Against this and
All other wars
For setting things right
Has always been our cause
These challenges – His Work
Cannot go ignored
For inherited in this His Life's Blood
Is the ability

Regardless of the volume of these

Ear-splitting roars

Or the height and force

Of raging floods

Every river, in His name, will be forded

And doves will forever soar

As onward Christian Soldiers...

gregorye.douglas
five/twenty-eight/cleareyesight

The B Side

In all of recorded history
There has never been a time
When store owners
Have requested
Or
Even begged
Black Men
To put on masks
Before entering...??!!

gregorye.douglas
four/twenty-four/cleareyesight

Juneteenth 20/20 –
Like Your Life Is Perishable...

the reason to celebrate
a freedom that was announced two years late
certainly today won't negate
this Covid Virus we've come to hate

reasoning should be reasonable
social seasoning make it feasible
that we need to tone down
this year's 19th just in order to be around

this Trump virus trumps this Juneteenth Celebration
yes across the entire face of this nation
consider the peril that you're facing
families in crowds don't give 6 feet of spacing

with strawberry soda and barbecue
and a mask on your face what will you do
Take it off maybe and throw it away

because of this very special celebration day

Today is a most important day
I'm not asking the celebration to go ignored
What I am sincerely really trying to say is
We Don't Need to See You in the ICU Ward

We've seen too many of us through plexiglass
On ventilators and fading fast
Pump your brakes and use caution
Use social distancing and keep your masks on

The Conspiracy Theory:
It's like playing chicken and they dare you to flinch
some will take the bait that's a cinch
and tomorrow's numbers may numb you
yes you might be numbed from some of the stats
others from the corpses that need to be viewed – Damn

gregorye.douglas
six/nineteen/cleareyesight

Fiction and Fact
The Questions of Donald Trump's Genius
in Evidence

How does and applicant who just walked through the
wrong door after failing to land
A White House janitorial job...??????!

What do you call someone who can fool
most of the people
all of the time????!

Confederate Monuments
and Civil War Battlefields

Perhaps it's a conscience thing, trump stepping up to try and preserve the confederate monuments. His conscience presenting itself as his reparations for ducking the Vietnam War for certainly the reason of his deferment (bone spurs) has in no way hampered his golf game at least in its frequency.

As of Oct 2019, trump incurred about 109 million dollars in taxpayer spending related to his golf outings (search snopes.com) and the games go on. The men on the monuments that trump attempts to defend in their time demonstrated more valor and dedication then trump could never be accused of, not even by himself.

Still these confederate monuments represent soldiers who lost the Civil War 155 years ago. Their depiction as heroes is a farce as trump himself will tell you; just like John McCain as a prisoner of war could not be considered a hero. Those monuments are subtle reminders to whites of ancestral comfort in better times and reinforces their supposed inherent right of privilege. To blacks these monuments are subliminal reinforcement of the ancestral separation, tyranny, oppression, blood harvests and deaths that whites commanded.

Today these structures are the needle in the compass pointing back in time. With tunnel vision, some whites will still look upon those times with more regard than the contributions that blacks have made post-Civil War that have vastly improved living conditions in these United States for all.

The United States has even landed on the moon because of black brilliance. We are allotted but 28 days in February, the shortest month of the year, to showcase the advantages that black advancement has aided in this nation's development and even the world's.

These rebel monuments are on display every day, and what advancements have they contributed to black people, in furthering the cause of this country? Every day on display and for what other cause? Move them to a monument park or a museum dedicated to the history of the confederacy.

As far as the Civil War battlefields are concerned,
leave them the hell alone and intact. They are ours as
much as they are yours. We fought there, we bled there,
and we died there. It was there on those battlefields
that we fought for our freedoms and it was there that
our courage and valor could not be hidden or denied
but was in the light of day and the darkness of night –
validated. From the first wars that this black skin fought,
still some whites have failed to understand and are still
reticent to see us as an ally and as an equal, even
though we have laid down our lives for this country from
the first war going forward.

Frankly, this poor representation of a president (45)
has shown neither conscience nor valor. He doesn't
have the grit for either. His ignorance and ego made the
swamp a cesspool. What followed on his watch was
more people died from a virus in a few months than
during the years of the Vietnam Conflict. 126,000 of
us blacks, reds, yellows, browns and yes, whites have
died.

He remains unapologetic about his miscalculation. The
strength of his administration lies in the people that we
elected that do not have our interest at heart – just

their Fuhrer's And in the face of this crumbling
disaster, trump comes at you to broker a deal for your
vote by trying to raise the southern monuments again.
This gambit is only to gain your vote but in no way,
shape or form will it Make America Great Again. It will
finally gut the American way of life. General Robert E.
Lee could see this and didn't – because he was a
considerate and honorable man.

gregorye.douglas
six/twenty-seven/cleareyesight

Aunt Elizabeth (1915 – 2016)

We all must make some sense of it
To know exactly where we fit
Then bravely endure this gravity
Until at last He sets us free

Free to loose these earthly bonds
To finally liberate a slave's laughter
Then stomping and dancing in bare feet
Hugging and kissing all that we meet

For one hundred years – a century
Imagine the changes that she'd see
From paths to roads to city streets
Wood stoves to Woolworth's counter treats

From kerosene to neon
From radio to T.V. and beyond
From segregation to integration
From no vote to a Black Man running this Nation

All at a price that she had paid
As smart as she was – she could only be a maid
She rode black's scar – a scab covered her pain
That wrenched her gut and tortured her brain

Their maid – my Monarch perfectly in control
Until Friday evenings when Seagrams loosed her soul
And the ghosts were as real as she is to me
And she tried to exorcise them to reclaim her sanity

On Mondays she hid both ghosts and her wishes
While in uniform she mopped, cooked, did the dishes
Ideas were kept secret – stored in her head
Ideas that went hungry and never were fed

Was Elizabeth ever really a child
Was there ever enough freedom for her to run wild
Did she just live like the tides of the sea
Or did she live through us – her family

We must all make some sense of it
To know exactly where we fit
The bravely endure this gravity

Until at last He sets us free...

gregorye.douglas/four/six/2016

The Color of Chaos
and its Burdens

In Slavery
When Blacks were condemned
And considered less than human
What kind of animal
Was the white
Who bred himself
Into his own
"Black Live Stock"
Now when he peers
Into their eyes
Imagine what he sees
Victims from his past
Casualties from his disease
Posed and even cast as
Hostages from his curse
Giving up his white wife's babies
For his black children to nurse
And worse
Hanging some of his children
Framed as "Strange Fruit" for all to see

Certainly not the best of him
Nor the worst of me
His eyes, my nose
His pigment in my skin
All
Struggle to be free!!!

gregorye.douglas
two/ten/twentyfifteen

Weather Worn White

having eyes
Eyes have seen
that as
the Color
of your
skin reflects
the content
of your
soul's reflex
its White
has lost
its purity
as it has
throughout
its history
and
progressively
has marked

your id
as
indelibly
dingy

gregoryedouglas
five/fourteen/2020

Yes

there are variations
on a theme
where our assassinations
are the sights
at the scenes
there's only one reason
why they couldn't stay
these MFs couldn't put
their hatred away
same as your justice
plays out for us
it digs up a verdict
and buries our trust

The Darkness in the Keyhole

If the true wealth of the black mind
Were actually placed on display
The world would have to
Stand and applaud
Perhaps even question
The color of their lord

What could they honestly say
Knowing that burdened black minds
Had performed in such extraordinary ways
Most silenced for their stolen ideas
Tearless pain yet pain-filled still stinging for years

Dr. Charles R. Drew of international mention
Died from life's most cruelest deaths
Being deprived of the use of his very invention
Last drop of his blood extinguished his last breath
While he perpetuated life for others

gregorye.douglas
two/twenty-nine/cleareyesight

Street Life Blueprint for Denzel

These young dead black men
are not heroes in the streets
they are just the victims
the casualties that death greets
there is no honor for these boys
who played with these grown -up toys
that did more than just make noise
it covered the lives which it destroys

With just five pounds of pressure
over and over and over
instead of the secrets they could discover
A book's hard covers are there to protect
its treasures they never had the curiosity to inspect
yet crowded in a pod they look for respect
although they were smart they didn't have the heart
to find the courage to grow apart
to find the courage to trust time
consistently making the wrong decisions.
Stomped stumped hearts don't grow
They only breed pain as their religion

From a street's education to seek relief

it's only brief before the wreath

Morphed into madness' darkest decision

In the darkness a glint of bling

The silent notorious signaling nod

Then the ear-piercing sound of that rod…and plants

them further into the dark

Breathe

I want to be able to greet and hold you

when you have met your goals

i want to shake your hand

knowing that your soul was never sold

first, i am hoping that you will outlast

another nightmare's forecast

where you can hear all the approaching screams

as a flash reflection heads in your direction

now your blood is spurting all over the streets

and the screams getting louder are only there to greet

your last breath trying to steal tomorrow…

gregoryedouglas/cleareyesight

Urban Renewal

Yes Stephon Clark
Was a troubled young Brother
But he should be here today
Hysterical fire is what Sac hired
Smothering bullets took his life away

Now what the Sac D.A. seems to say
Is that Stephon in his own way
Wanted to be euthanized so in an act of suicide
Excepted death as mercy's prize
And in a flash went out that way

You see it can't be fixed now
You just can't put life back
Into his dead body somehow
And just command him to breathe
So what does this leave

It leaves a lie
That has made blind justice a prostitute
Creating for Sac's altered conscience a substitute
Saying it's ok to stuff all of those
Dead black bodies into potholes
To make all city streets smoother

gregorye.douglas
three/six/2019

Open Season

...And my fate
regardless of the statements
that I make
Or positions that I take
hands up, behind my back,
draped over a car or prostrate...

This natural ebony pelt is a badge
carrying with it the same old adage:
that I am a black body bullseye
and there should be no surprise
when I become a lead receptacle
a spectacle for my family to see
riddled in riddles that are designed
to kill me and let my killer go free

they always manage
to play me as the disadvantaged
because my neighborhood

paints a psychological profile
that labels me as hostile
even when walking away
or even kneeling to pray
and what did they say

"I feared for my life"
when you never feared for mine
you told them, "there was no time"
You might as well have
patiently stood us up in a firing line
and shot us all – this to remind
the relatives of the dead
that they are second-class

these cops first cover their ass
even when we are weaponless
if there is a flash but no report
then they open up their season of blood sport

Then call for back-up
and partner with the court
to confirm that black lives were
always meant for sport

always meant to be short
second-class and meaningless
a special kind of justice
That frees these villains but never us
in a verdict of ashes... to dust

It must be quite a thrill
a superhero to kill
it took nineteen shots
to bring him to the ground
"I'm hyped at the sight
Oh, he didn't fire a round!
didn't even fight?
But the flash should save my ass
Hell it's just another "N" down
How many does that make anyway
did anyone check with the EPA?
We need to hang those skins
like notices on the courthouse door
It used to be from trees back then
But we don't do that anymore"
Looking backward to another year

gregorye.douglas
three/five/2019

These Are Times That Try Black Men's Souls

If this was a scene demonstrating law enforcement with subduing a rabid dog or knife-wielding or gun-wielding irrational uncooperative citizen, then perhaps, just perhaps what transpired could be seen as a consequence of that struggle to defend the public. But this citizen was cooperative, this citizen was not combative, this citizen did not have a weapon, this citizen was not ranting or raving, this citizen was not demonstrating, this citizen was not involved in an argument or altercation, this citizen was just Black.

George Floyd's Black skin and that alone precipitated the events that led to his death. With the full weight of the officer's knee on Mr. Floyd's neck, I suspect that this was the latest in police submission tactics and it certainly was effective. Perhaps this officer of the law was not bilingual or versed in Swahili and didn't understand the Swahili term "I can't breathe!" Oh, that's right! Mr. Floyd spoke in perfect English!

How is Mr. Floyd expected to arise and get into a vehicle with the full weight of his oppressor still on his neck? And why the hell wouldn't Mr. Dudley let Mr. Flood get up or was he anticipating the sound of a snap while he continued to occupy his alternative choke position?!

This is racism plain and simple in full view. And his posse, whose greatest deed that day must have been to correctly button their shirts, demonstrated the collective IQ of 9. These imbeciles stood around like hyenas holding off outsiders while waiting for the end to come; an end that resulted in the Senseless Death of another Black Man. My greatest fear is for the next Black Man who is stopped. Justice in these cases continues to be something meted out by the blind and the deaf. It's far past time to cancel this Hunting Season but courts continue to license it.

gregorye.douglas
five/twenty-eight/cleareysight

The Parallax View

Covid-19 is to blame
for confining us
in front of the screen
that on either side
played it out over and over again
and both of its sides had captured me
as horror exploded right through
the screen of my smart tv
as I inhaled all the air coming out of his lungs
and in that moment we both had become
the carnage... at least until my next breath
it choked George fast
it choked George slow
for 8 min and 46 sec George wouldn't go
it ran so vividly
that I didn't know
where I was... on which side of the screen
I knew I'd cried out at the site of this scene
Stop! Stop!

Me not knowing in that spit second
where I actually was
had I put it on freeze

my heart would stop
then race at the same pace
retracing his breathing
in each moment
attempting in each frame
to discover before poor George's
air became
the air he donated let's give it a name
exhausted
he donated his last breath to me
allowing my mind to catch up and find
and to free my voice
refusing to pause I made my choice

Stop! Stop!
but how loud had I turned up the volume
enough to be heard through the crowd
not enough for that damned cop on his neck
not giving George or me or the crowd the respect to
Stop! Stop!

forever to remember
more than the leaves changing in September
were his racists eyes glazed over
like a shark for the kill
ignoring the spirit of one man's life soaring

having been forced right out of his chest
he enjoyed the thrill that his hate was causing
oblivious to everyone else's distress
here, I'm still sitting on both sides of this scene
trying to understand who I am what I've been
And how I feel about humanity
And what will my children feel when they think about me
Stop? Stop!

gregorye.douglas
six/seventeen/cleareyesight

Who Made Black Guilty?

Who made Black guilty?
Justice remains white
We have seen it in the daytime
And we witnessed it at night
Photographic scenes like this
Yesterday were always missed
Today it should have been decay
Still others content with its history
Continue producing this misery
Leaving relations to slowly rot away

Who made Black guilty?
Before Blacks would bleed
Now knees intercede
With the same effect
All to do their part
One choking poor George's neck
Both penetrating our hearts

And by those sworn
To protect the innocent
By what means
Are these laws being bent

Who made Black guilty?
This in the face of peace
Are we the overwhelming opposition
As Blacks
To take up offensive positions
Of hands up
Of on our knees
Of draped over the hood
Or thrown on the ground
Setting us up... like sitting ducks
Before we are put down

Who made Black guilty?
There wasn't a damned thing that he said
George Floyd's wind was robbed from him
Leaving another Black man dead
Revisited again is this Strange Fruit
Not dangling from an old tree
Nor caused by the noose or even his gravity

But caused by what all of us could see

At its root was the Full Weight of a body

Exerted through his Knee

May the Black prisoner who now is set free

Haunt his white oppressor on land, by air and at sea –

daily

Breathe, George, breathe real hot breaths

Down upon his neck and never ever leave him to forget

Who made Black guilty...

gregorye.douglas
six/five/cleareyesight

Minneapolis Mean: The Definition of Justice

To the enraged protesters
in this "injustice boil"
this has been allowed to simmer
over hundreds of years
still leaves blacks with nothing at all
except coffins and acid in their tears
in the courts
the deaf and the mute report
simply to occupy the chairs
finding nothing wrong with "each event"
always "the blue" is innocent
ignoring black bodies bullet rent
then thanking themselves for the time spent

And this is called Justice
it just disgusts us
the reason for our rage
is that black deaths
are condoned at any age
and judicial time is purposely staged
to soften and cool the offenses
yes until it's so sublime, yes almost even senseless

like using a condom
in a sexual attack negates "rape"
roll the offense back ~ perhaps the key to escape
yes ~ is time
this Justice serves
to widen the divide
for their avenue of escape and to separate and hide

Black freedom's ~ a low regard
and looking over the fence
at the same white offenses
makes it increasingly hard
to disregard what is meant
by reason of white/black intent
for by the same process
Blacks are sent
to cemeteries and prisons
for the same crimes or incidents
not meriting the same white decisions
do not come to the same conclusions
that further enrages us
about your white delusions
that all men are created equal
that in your god we can trust

and we've seen its sequel
over and over again
no longer hidden
even when body-cam driven
scenes upon scenes as they kill us
just enrages and disgusts us
and you're asking for more time
why? To commit more crimes
over decades and over centuries are spread
hundreds and thousands of Black Bodies Dead
hung and burned and bullet-ridden
smashed and disemboweled with souvenirs given

here and now your Justice is winning
but Justice – we can no longer provide this
wanton Black thinning
you sit here and ask us for more time
aren't centuries not enough
For all the Blacks that we find
the Blacks that you have snuffed
What time?
Is it Time to get it right???
When these crimes are committed in plain sight?

is it time to rid the jury of earplugs and masks?
is it the time you thought we'd forget the past?
or is it the space created just to cover your white ass?
because presently that is what justice is.

Blood of my brothers grew this nation and that with
their faces down
Rewarded now with a knee in the neck just to keep them
there...
How Blind Is Your White?!
How Black Is Your Soul?!!

gregorye.douglas
five/thirty?/cleareyesight

Trump Trips in Tulsa?
Perhaps Avoiding
the Ventilator

So you made your decision
And joined the Donald Trump religion
Because you think he walks on water
When he's really just on the floor
His rudeness and ignorance
All of you choose to ignore

Trump will risk you, his fan base
Not even requesting a mask for your face
All for just one thing – your vote
Which can never be expressed
With a ventilator in your throat
Trump's winning at all costs
Is all at your expense
He's not the next Jesus
He's not here to please us
Your boss –

Hides the cape the devil sent
Has his wardrobe finally been spent?

One hundred and thirteen thousand nine hundred and
fourteen U.S. deaths
Going to skip this?
Isn't that enough to take your breath??
Or does it actually take yours to convince you??!!

gregorye.douglas
six/twenty/cleareyesight

8 Min. 46 Sec.

Under the auspices of token justice and laws
Black hatred and rage have been contained and
controlled.
While the Rhetoric and rationalizations proceed, they
only
disguise the true deep-seated motive for these Military
Ops
and that is to decapitate the Black Race.
The proof lies in America's refusal to amend its
greatest go
to word "justice" and by not enacting laws that focus on
the
elimination of malicious violence acts against Blacks,

The proof also lies in this country's inability to allow
the successful
assimilation of Blacks into "the land of milk and honey"
through

nationally unfettered voter registration and meaningful educational
opportunities along with jobs that pay well and have futures for
advancement.

The echoes from the closing of Mr. George Floyd's coffin should
immediately lead us to the courthouse doors to rectify these
inequities. It is as clear as the eight minutes and forty-six
seconds that deprived us of a Black Man, a father, a disciplinarian
and a friend. Gone in 8 Min. 46 Sec.... and taking with him our
breath and our senses - until when????

gregorye.douglas
six/nine/ clear eyesight

A Renaissance in dynamic thinking
Could simply start with
The designation of
A new name and hue for
The White House

The Way of the Warrior
1940 * Rep. John Robert Lewis * 2020

He should have been a headline
But always seemed a footnote
Until you imagine yourself
Walking in his shoes
Tired, trod upon
Bitten, battered and bloodied
But in his footprint
Was summoned from this gnome
The incredulous amount of
Courage, Determination and Power
That IT must have taken
Just to make his very next step...
And now those that we take
So very much easier
Like Hansel and Gretel's crumbs
Looking up from his footprints
This star's half-life
Is Heaven's milestone

gregoryedouglas
seven/twenty/cleareyesight

I hope that "On the Other Side of This Reality" has been both interesting and insightful. If this read has been thoroughly enjoyable then I, as its author, have missed my Mark.

gregoryedouglas
eight/six/cleareyesight

www.ingramcontent.com/pod-product-compliance
Lightning Source LLC
Chambersburg PA
CBHW060638280326
41933CB00012B/2081